America's

PROTECTING

Redrock

A NATIONAL

Wilderness

TREASURE

SOUTHERN UTAH WILDERNESS ALLIANCE

I. CANYONS WITHOUT END On a hot August day in 1935, at a remote ranch south of the little town of Caineville, Utah, two men secure the hitches on their pack horses and set out to the east. The country ahead — full of dry washes, impassable cliffs, wildly contorted canyons — is the largest remaining roadless tract in the lower 48 states.

Five weeks and hundreds of miles later the men, H. Dodge Freeman of Chicago and David Rust of Provo, Utah, complete their journey, a broad circuit of the canyon lands. They have traversed the Henry Mountains, the Dirty Devil River, White Canyon, much of present-day Canyonlands National Park, and Labyrinth Canyon on the Green River. This trip is the culmination of years of exploring the canyon country. Freeman wrote of his adventures the next year, in a letter to the Moab *Times-Independent*:

> *I have spent 4 of the greatest summers of my life in the slickrocks of southeastern Utah and I feel certain that nothing quite so inspiring and intriguing can exist anywhere else on earth.*

Midway through their journey, the two adventurers stopped by Natural Bridges National Monument, a tiny protected enclave in the heart of this wild region. There they met Zeke Johnson, a veteran guide and caretaker of the monument. An enthusiastic promoter of the canyon country's scenic wonders, Johnson told them of the Park Service's plans to create a 4.5-million-acre Escalante National Monument, encompassing much of the wild land they had crossed.

3

ABOVE: **Dodge Freeman entering the badlands north of the Henry Mountains at the start of his 1935 trip with David Rust. South Caineville Mesa is in the background.**
OPPOSITE: **Factory Butte casts a sundial spike across the vast badlands south of the San Rafael Swell.**

RAY WHEELER

The White Cliffs of the Upper Kanab Creek proposed wilderness area. Decades of roadbuilding and other development have isolated this area from nearby wildlands in the upper Paria River drainage. In the 1980s, a proposal for a coal slurry line prompted the BLM to drop this area from wilderness consideration. The new Grand Staircase-Escalante National Monument covers part of the area, but wilderness designation of the entire Upper Kanab Creek roadless area is needed.

Freeman was one of the very few who had seen much of this proposed monument. But he worried that a new park would bring with it new highways and intensive tourist development:

> It has always been encouraging to me to know that out there in your country there lies one large area, at least, that represents something wild and remote, even in the material days we are living in at present. What a pity it would be to destroy this — even to touch it. Why shouldn't the government take steps to preserve such a territory by forbidding roads to enter it, just as it takes steps to create national parks for the opposite reason?

DAVID MUENCH

5

Freeman was arguing, in effect, for the concept of "wilderness" — something the government would take three decades to officially embrace in the Wilderness Act of 1964.

Freeman's concern about the proposed Escalante National Monument seems strange today, when our national parks and monuments are among the most zealously protected lands. Such was not the case in the 1930s. The National Park Service, fighting for recognition among the "progressive" bureaucracies of the New Deal, saw road building and tourist development as part of its mission. New parks and monuments, agency leaders felt, should be made accessible to an American public that was developing a passion

Where the San Rafael River exits the gorge known as the Little Grand Canyon, the rimrocks recede and a series of grand buttes and mesas take the foreground. It is all wild country — but only the Citizens' Proposal would protect this outstanding monolith, called Assembly Hall Peak.

for automobile touring. Recreation roads counted as public works projects to help boost the country out of the Great Depression.

The tourist potential of the canyon country was not lost on Utah officials. In 1936, the Utah State Planning Board endorsed the concept of new park designations in the canyon lands. The Escalante National Monument proposal even won endorsement from the Moab Lions Club, which felt that the monument would "immediately bring southeastern Utah to the front as a tourist playground."

Opposition to the monument from grazing, mining and hydropower interests prompted the Park Service to propose a smaller monument with fewer restrictions on development. By 1940, this abbreviated proposal gained Interior Secretary Harold Ickes's approval and stood ready for Presidential proclamation.

II. THE WILDERNESS IDEA At the same time that the National Park Service was promoting the Escalante National Monument, a handful of concerned individuals were calling attention to the steady attrition of the nation's wild places. Robert Marshall, a New York-born forester and wilderness explorer, was the most vocal of these visionaries. In 1936, he attempted to assess just how many large areas of wilderness were left in the lower 48 states. He estimated that a roadless area of 8,890,000 acres remained in the canyon country of Utah and northern Arizona. This was the largest single roadless tract anywhere in the country, and included the terrain proposed for the Escalante monument. Marshall called for immediate government action to protect these large wilderness expanses. In an article accompanying his wilderness inventory (published in *The Living Wilderness* in November, 1936), he wrote:

> *All over the country, people are beginning to protest in a concerted manner against the invasion of roadless tracts by routes of modern transportation. Encouragingly enough, a number of these protests have been heeded, and several splendid roadless areas have thus been saved . . . Yet others, unfortunately, have been invaded either because nobody happened to realize that invasion was imminent, or because no one was aware that there was a significant area to be saved.*

For the canyon country of Utah, Marshall's words — and Freeman's — were prophetic.

The Labyrinth Canyon on the Green River. Wilderness proposals by the BLM and Utah's Congressional delegation would protect only part of this river canyon, the float down which was called a "delightful journey" by Barry Goldwater in 1940. The Citizens' Proposal takes in the entire canyon and surrounding wild lands.

Love it, hate it, or ignore it, wilderness is in our American soul, and we are loath to give it up, or see it become so diminished, so vestigial, that it ceases to be what it has always been to us —those cussed, godforsaken, dangerous patches of outback full of things that can kill us.

Donald Snow

"It does not matter in the slightest that only a few people every year will go into it. That is precisely its value. Roads would be a desecration, crowds would ruin it." — Wallace Stegner, from a letter written in 1960 to a Federal recreation planning board. He was speaking of the unprotected wild lands east of Capitol Reef National Park, of which the Red Desert country shown here is among the most forbidding.

JEFF GARTON

FIFTY YEARS OF DEVELOPING THE CANYON LANDS

Five decades of development (white areas on map) have fragmented and reduced the wild lands of Utah's canyon country.

At the end of World War Two, most of southern Utah's public lands were still roadless and undeveloped. Primitive tracks led down toward the Colorado River but were frequently impassable. Not until 1946 were roads completed and a ferry crossing installed at the tiny outpost of Hite.

Within ten years, however, uranium prospectors, spurred by government price supports, had gouged thousands of miles of roads and tracks into the backcountry. Subsequent mineral exploration booms in the 1970s and 1980s further reduced the wilderness, and Lake Powell flooded Glen Canyon, the finest canyon of all. The result? A diminished and fragmented, though still magnificent, wild region.

Today, large areas have been protected within national parks, but wilderness designation is needed for millions of acres of BLM wild lands outside of the parks. Even the fate of the new Grand Staircase-Escalante National Monument is uncertain; will its 1.5 million acres of wildlands remain undeveloped?

RAY WHEELER

The postwar era brought an intensive search for oil, gas, and uranium to the wild lands of southern Utah. Perhaps the upper Escalante River drainage on the Kaiparowits Plateau (shown here) had to be sacrificed to fuel the nation's growth. But can a line now be drawn, and society say, "Enough?"

1945

1998

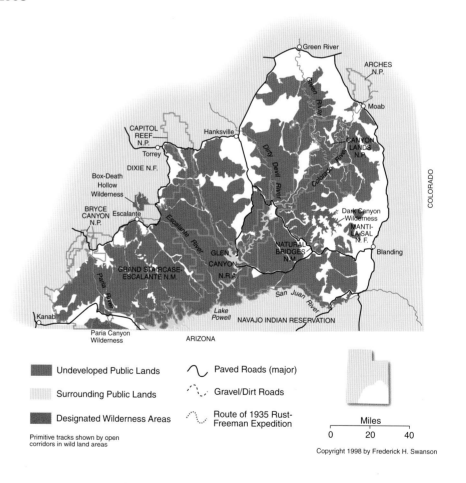

Undeveloped Public Lands		Paved Roads (major)
Surrounding Public Lands		Gravel/Dirt Roads
Designated Wilderness Areas		Route of 1935 Rust-Freeman Expedition

Primitive tracks shown by open corridors in wild land areas

Miles
0   20   40

Copyright 1998 by Frederick H. Swanson

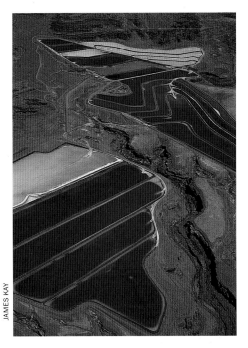

JAMES KAY

III. DISMEMBERING A WILDERNESS

The Escalante National Monument proposal was sidetracked by World War Two and was never seriously reconsidered during the postwar development boom. Left to the Bureau of Land Management's administration, the roadbuilding that ensued in the canyon country exceeded anything the Park Service might have done. In the early 1950s, the Atomic Energy Commission let contracts for a thousand miles of uranium exploration roads in southern Utah. The Federal Highway Administration paid for major highway projects across the canyon lands. And the Bureau of Reclamation spent $300 million to build Glen Canyon Dam and flood hundreds of miles of the Colorado River and its side canyons.

Few protested the gradual attrition of this great wilderness during the postwar years. One of the first was Ward Roylance, a Utahn who in the years following the war set out with his brother in a series of rattletrap vehicles to explore the canyon country. By the late 1960s he was evangelizing the Colorado Plateau in homemade natural-history films, slide shows and self-published magazines. Roylance's writings are filled with wonder and delight as he discovered the scenic gems of the canyon country. Increasingly, however, he was saddened by the steady push for development. When huge potash evaporation ponds were built directly under his beloved Dead Horse Point, he wrote:

> For me the ponds had removed something precious
> from my life. Never since have I been able to glance
> more than momentarily in their direction the very
> few times I have returned to the point.

Roylance repeatedly warned of the need for a comprehensive approach to planning the future of this region. Otherwise, he believed, (writing in 1971):

> [W]e see a sad vision of the former Enchanted
> Wilderness, no longer deserving of such a name. In our
> vision it has become a combination amusement and
> industrial park. Paved highways spiderweb the land.
> Rural valleys and mountain slopes are dotted with
> campgrounds, trailer villages and summer homes.
> Skies are marred by jet trails, industrial plumes and
> smog. The erstwhile primeval silence is shattered by
> the roar of planes, helicopters, cycles, boats, mining
> machines, power plants, trucks, cars and noisy voices.

ABOVE: **Ward Roylance first toured the canyon country in 1942 and his appreciation for the land only deepened with each passing decade (photo dated 1958, photographer unknown).** TOP: **Of the potash ponds that scarred the vista from Dead Horse Point in 1971, Roylance wrote: "Americans in general, and Utahns in particular, were not easily aroused enmasse — in those days — in opposition to such developments in pristine wilderness." They are now, Ward, in part thanks to your visionary efforts.**

11

12

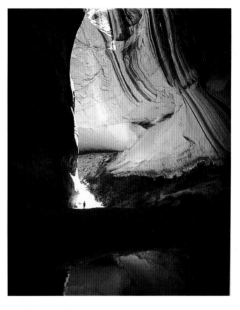

OPPOSITE: Sandstone cave near Arches National Park. Search the canyon country long enough and you will encounter wonders not found in any guidebook. The chance to discover places such as this — and to be rewarded for one's personal effort — is vanishing from the American scene. RIGHT: Cathedral in the Desert in Glen Canyon. Photo taken in 1962 by W.L. Rusho, courtesy of U.S. Bureau of Reclamation. BELOW: Ken Sleight, veteran Utah backcountry and river guide (photographer unknown).

IV. ONE LAST OPPORTUNITY Today, many of the changes that Freeman, Marshall and Roylance feared have taken place. Government agencies continue to advance proposals that would complete the destruction. But many new voices have come to the aid of Utah's wild lands. At public meetings held by Governor Mike Leavitt and Utah's Congressional delegation in 1995, hundreds of Utahns from all parts of the state voiced their opposition to the continuing destruction of wilderness. We can hear in their voices the same thread of concern that goes back sixty years.

The wild canyon country of the 1930s has been sadly diminished. But if we act with foresight, a great piece of the original American wilderness can still be protected for our future. It can be done without jeopardizing the livelihoods of local residents, although they will have to let go of dreams of great wealth from another government-subsidized development boom.

Those dreams were largely false anyway. Fifty years of massive federal intervention has brought neither wealth nor stability to local communities. Construction jobs were temporary and mostly went to out-of-staters. So did the mineral wealth and hydropower. Many local residents now realize that the Fed's development schemes were never meant to benefit them.

Is there some compromise that will support a sustainable local economy — and protect what is left of this great wilderness? There is, but only if we abandon the mega-development dreams that have held sway for the last half-century, and look to the promise that wilderness holds for the future.

I have been fortunate that I have had the opportunity to enjoy the wilderness lands of the canyon country for most of my life. We once had beautiful lands — we had Music Temple, we had Cathedral in the Desert, Gregory Natural Bridge. Now these forms are all under water. A great wilderness area was taken away from us, buried under hundreds of feet of water. We have very few real wilderness lands left. They are priceless to us.

Ken Sleight
San Juan County, Utah
Governor Leavitt's
wilderness hearings,
April 1995

If we do not deliberately protect our remaining wilderness in Utah, I fear it will eventually disappear. It will not vanish through beneficial development, but will instead be lost through gradual attrition for no good reason at all. Having been born in southern Utah and having spent my youth in its unmatchable canyons and forests, I want to ensure that the same opportunity will be available for future generations.

Wayne Owens
*Author of H.R. 1500
Member of Congress
Utah Second District
1972-1974; 1986-1992*

14

The Book Cliffs is one of the world's longest escarpments. Behind it, the harsh lowland desert gives way to montane forests that support abundant wildlife.

TOM TILL

I've been living in southern Utah 18 years after being born and raised in Davis County. This was before it became one big subdivision like wilderness opponents want to create here in southwestern Utah. I'm here to disprove the lie that local people don't want wilderness . . . The truth is that most southern Utahns are frightened by runaway growth and want to see as much land protected from development as possible.

Linda Wood
Cedar City, Utah
Governor Leavitt's wilderness hearings, April 1995

SCOTT GROENE

17

OPPOSITE: Mt. Ellen in the Henry Mountains supports a pleasant forest of aspen and fir — contrasting with the badlands that surround this mountain range. Scenery and recreation are well-known uses of wilderness, but protecting plant and animal communities is just as crucial. One such area is found on Bridger Jack Mesa (LEFT) near Canyonlands National Park. These areas are among the few desert landscapes that have escaped wholesale alteration of their natural habitats. ABOVE: Indiscriminate off-road vehicle use disturbs more than the desert silences — it pounds down the fragile desert soil crusts that support an unbelievable array of highly adapted plants and animals.

18

I'm a Carbon County native. I currently live in Salt Lake City. Fifty years ago, we had 16 to 18 million acres of wilderness. In my lifetime I've seen two-thirds of that wiped out. Gone. We've only got just under six million acres left. We need to be protecting it. I want to enjoy these lands with my grandchildren the way I enjoyed them with my parents and with my grandparents.

Gail Hoskisson
Salt Lake City, Utah
Governor Leavitt's
wilderness hearings,
April 1995

This compromise is already in place, on the ground. Many of the canyon country's highways and jeep trails should probably never have been built, but there they are. Now Mom and Pop can see Utah's greatest natural spectacles from a recreational vehicle. Jeep enthusiasts can explore hundreds of miles of scenic backcountry routes. Fortunately, hikers, backpackers and river runners can still thrill to discovering the farthest reaches of the canyons.

Why not a moratorium? Let's declare victory — the canyon lands of Utah are now available for everyone to enjoy. Tourism of all flavors is proving to be a major economic asset in the canyon country of Utah. **So let's keep the rest of the wilderness intact.** Within the boundaries of the remaining wild areas, let us build no more roads. No more power lines, no more mining pits, and most difficult of all — no more boom-time dreams. That is the principle behind the Citizens' Proposal for America's Redrock Wilderness — a proposal developed by people familiar with the land and endorsed by the 156 member organizations of the Utah Wilderness Coalition.

OPPOSITE: **Jones Bench in the San Rafael Swell is so remote, it would be easy to overlook it in the political debates over wilderness designation. But that would be a shame, for this area is an important transition zone between the forested High Plateaus of central Utah and the arid moonscapes of the Salt Wash desert to the east. Such transition zones are especially important for migratory wildlife.** TOP: **The White River proposed wilderness area in the Uinta Basin of northeastern Utah.** BOTTOM: **Places that let the spirit soar: rainwater pool in the sandstone expanse of Mancos Mesa, Cedar Mesa region.**

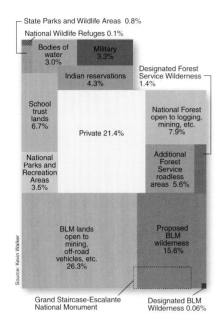

State Parks and Wildlife Areas 0.8%

National Wildlife Refuges 0.1%

Bodies of water 3.0%

Military 3.3%

Indian reservations 4.3%

Designated Forest Service Wilderness 1.4%

School trust lands 6.7%

Private 21.4%

National Forest open to logging, mining, etc. 7.9%

National Parks and Recreation Areas 3.5%

Additional Forest Service roadless areas 5.6%

BLM lands open to mining, off-road vehicles, etc. 26.3%

Proposed BLM wilderness 15.6%

Grand Staircase-Escalante National Monument

Designated BLM Wilderness 0.06%

THE BALANCE OF WILDERNESS IN UTAH

**The compromise is already in place:
the 16 percent of Utah's BLM lands that are still
wild should remain so.**

TOP: **Few people venture out
into the lonely hills of Nokai
Dome in southeastern Utah's
Cedar Mesa. Must this fact
alone doom its future as
wilderness?** BOTTOM: **The
desert tortoise symbolizes the
dependence of wildlife on
undisturbed habitat.**

21

Protecting the wilderness is never the easy thing. We can continue as we always have, building another road here and another dam there, until one day we remember with an inner ache that "there used to be some great country here."

For sixty years, people have spoken out for the sake of the redrock wilderness. What were once a few isolated voices now number in the tens of thousands. Now, while there is still a great wild region left in southern Utah, is the time to heed those voices. While we still can, let us finally safeguard the wilderness.

The need to safeguard Utah's rich archeological resources such as this Cedar Mesa ruin led the Utah Professional Archeological Council to endorse the Citizens' Proposal for Redrock Wilderness. By restricting vehicle access, wilderness helps protect such sites from rampant vandalism and looting.

The Kaiparowits Plateau spans a huge sweep of wild country. The new Grand Staircase-Escalante National Monument has set aside most of the Plateau to protect "unique geological, paleontological, archeological, biological and historical values." Oil companies have been blading old, primitive tracks within the monument, and local county commissioners are set on paving roads to bring tourists. Wilderness designation within the monument lands is crucial to protect the region's wildness. INSET: The Cockscomb on the western edge of the Kaiparowits.

22

24

TOM MILLER

KAIPAROWITS PLATEAU

"The loneliest place in the Lower 48." That's what *Car and Driver* magazine called the Kaiparowits Plateau. They had a computer expert find the farthest point from a paved road or town in the lower 48 states — and came up with a point on Fiftymile Mountain at the eastern edge of the Kaiparowits.

How ironic—because major energy companies have long been trying to turn the Kaiparowits into one of the busiest, noisiest places in the rural West. First there was the gigantic Kaiparowits Power Project of the 1970s, which would have placed four huge coal-fired generators in the heart of the Plateau.

More recently, a foreign-owned firm wanted to mine Kaiparowits coal, truck it through Utah rural towns, and ship it to Pacific Rim countries.

Fortunately, on September 18, 1996, President Bill Clinton, responding to nationwide concern over the fate of this region, established a 1.7-million-acre Grand Staircase-Escalante National Monument that includes most of the Kaiparowits Plateau. While not specifically banning coal mining, the designation of the monument will likely preclude the roads and powerlines needed to mine coal. A bold step toward protecting this magnificent treasure, the new National Monument still needs the additional safeguard of wilderness designation to ensure that the region's scenic, biological and cultural resources are not damaged.

25

A wasteland to some, a place of inspiring beauty to others. The debate over the value of a 650,000-acre wilderness region such as the Kaiparowits Plateau is really a debate over the future direction of our society. Will all the last remote reaches of public lands be developed? Or will more than a token few small areas be set aside? OPPOSITE PAGE: The cliffs of Nipple Bench at the southern edge of the Grand Staircase-Escalante National Monument. THIS PAGE: Looking east from Smoky Mountain into Last Chance Creek in the proposed Burning Hills wilderness unit of the Kaiparowits region, also within the national monument.

WHITE CANYON/CEDAR MESA

Eight hundred years ago, the cliffs and plateaus of southeastern Utah were home to large bands of the Anasazi people. Benefitting from a cooler, wetter climate, they grew crops on the mesas and built their stone dwellings under the cliffs along winding, intricate canyons.

Today we marvel at what they left behind. Southeastern Utah has the highest concentration of ancient pueblo-style remains in the country, and more are being unearthed. One writer called the area a Library of Congress for the study of prehistory.

To some, though, this region is nothing more than an unlocked, unguarded storehouse. Vandalism and commercial pothunting have taken a heavy toll of most Anasazi sites. The best protection is afforded by wilderness — which restricts vehicle access.

Wilderness designation for the Cedar Mesa and White Canyon region will still allow proper scientific study of prehistoric remains. Land will still be available for traditional uses by native peoples, such as gathering firewood and pinyon nuts. And wilderness will give us all the chance to see this land much as it looked to its ancient inhabitants.

HARVEY HALPERN

PRECEDING: The ancient Anasazi people left hundreds of outstanding examples of pueblo-style architecture under cliffs and ledges of the Cedar Mesa region. Increasing human visitation, as well as ever-present looters and vandals, threaten these irreplaceable sites. By protecting remote sites within wilderness, we decrease the chances of inadvertent or malicious damage. ABOVE: The remote Nokai Dome area offers seldom-visited canyons carved into broad slickrock uplands. LEFT: Exploring Comb Ridge. OPPOSITE: One of the most challenging slot canyon hikes on the Colorado Plateau is found in lower White Canyon. Its tributaries are even less frequently explored.

STEWART AITCHISON

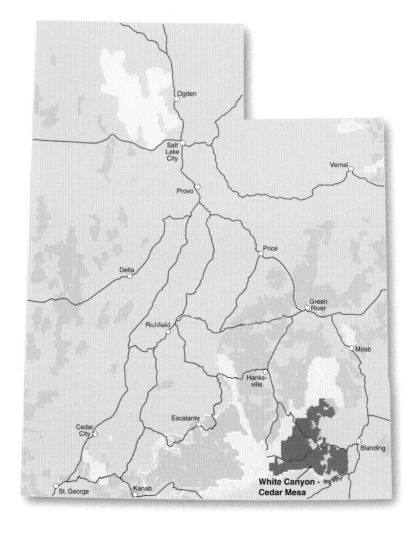

White Canyon - Cedar Mesa

JAMES KAY

STEPHEN TRIMBLE

Morning in the lower Dirty Devil River canyon. For ninety miles this shallow, muddy stream winds past sandstone domes and cliffs. Previous government proposals would have created a patchwork wilderness, protecting parts of the river corridor but omitting many miles of the main canyon and surrounding wild lands. Only the Citizens' Proposal recognizes the Dirty Devil country as an integral wilderness. INSET: Places of wonder and learning — exploring rainwater potholes in the Dirty Devil country.

JEFF GARTON

JAMES KAY

Happy Canyon narrows to a vivid slot just before it enters the Dirty Devil River. This area was left out of the Utah Congressional delegation's proposals in the 104th Congress. The rationale was remnants of old, eroding bulldozer tracks in the upper canyon, left by prospectors in the 1950s and early 1980s. The mining companies have yet to find anything of value. Should this landscape be held open on the chance they might someday make a strike? Or will the Dirty Devil country be recognized for what it already is — incomparable wilderness?

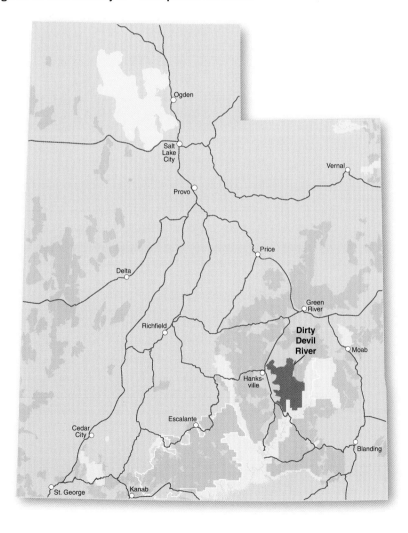

DIRTY DEVIL RIVER

A century ago, Butch Cassidy and the Wild Bunch took refuge in the side canyons of the Dirty Devil. Today, refugees from a crowded, mechanized world seek out this country. They find many wonders . . . a 90-mile wilderness float trip down the Dirty Devil River . . . jaw-dropping vistas overlooking Happy Canyon and Fiddler Butte . . . rare, relict plant communities on isolated mesa tops.

The Dirty Devil is part and parcel of the Canyonlands region, and probably should have been included in Canyonlands National Park. But for decades mining and energy companies have set their sights on the Dirty Devil. In the late 1970s, corporate uranium prospectors bladed dozens of miles of bulldozer tracks into the area. Plans were hatched for gigantic tar-sands recovery fields — industrial complexes of mind-boggling size, all on the doorstep of Canyonlands National Park. The transformation from wilderness to industrial zone was encouraged by the BLM, which allowed illegal roadbuilding within its wilderness study areas and carefully excised all potential mineral lands from its wilderness recommendations.

The energy boom fell through, and today the old 'dozer tracks, though still faintly visible, are returning to nature. Local county commissioners, however, want to establish "highway" rights-of-way along these tracks, keeping them open to vehicle use.

We say that the Dirty Devil country is wilderness and ought to stay that way. Close off the old bulldozer tracks, keep the canyons wild, let the grass grow over the old landing strips and well pads. The imprint of man, fading away within this vast region, is substantially unnoticeable. Wilderness is the highest and best use.

OPPOSITE: A handful of western wilderness rivers offer a quiet, easy float trip, uninterrupted by powerboats and highway roar. The Dirty Devil, when it is running deep enough, is one of the best.

33

SAN RAFAEL SWELL

If Utah had no Canyonlands, no Zion, Bryce or Arches national parks, the San Rafael Swell would surely be the state's proudest natural feature. For geology has run riot in the San Rafael Swell, creating jagged sawtooth ridges running for dozens of miles, bald sandstone domes rising straight out of high plateaus, a river gorge 1500 feet deep, and a mysterious badland expanse that turns back all but the most determined explorers.

Will we protect this awesome region as a whole, or merely carve it into a few isolated scenic fragments? The Bureau of Land Management and local development boosters concede that some of the Swell's scenic wonders should be protected. But the setting for the jewels is missing from their proposals. Take Mexican Mountain, for example. The cliff lines and plateaus west of this imposing monolith are missing from other wilderness proposals. Why? The BLM wants to keep these lands available for potential tar sands development. Should tar sands ever become economic to mine — and it's a long way from that — the land disturbance required to extract it is simply staggering. What is the value of setting aside a small wilderness area and then proposing a major industrial complex immediately next to it?

The southern reaches of the San Rafael Swell provide another example. There, the Muddy Creek-Salt Wash desert reaches south to Hanksville and Highway 24, penetrated by only a few primitive roads. It is a barren wasteland to some, but biologists marvel at the large number of specialized and rare plant species that live there. In turn, a remarkable variety of pollinating insects and bee species have evolved a close relationship with those plants. At the fringes of the Muddy Creek desert, off-road vehicles are already eroding soils and ripping up the native plant communities. If we allow more roads to be built into this region — as local authorities demand — more and more of these fragile biota will simply disappear.

STEVE HOWE

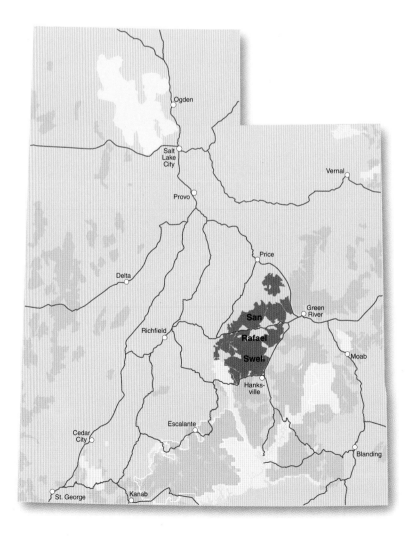

PREVIOUS: Storm over the northern San Rafael Swell. The classic erosional features of the San Rafael Swell are recognized internationally by geologists. Utah state planning officials recognized the area's stature as a scenic wonderland as far back as 1936. Even local county commissioners have endorsed some wilderness designations for the area. But only the Citizens' Proposal would fully protect the entire range of scenic, geological, recreational and biotic treasures found in the Swell. THIS PAGE: Datura or jimsonweed. The southern San Rafael Swell desert contains notable examples of relict plant communities. Wilderness designation helps prevent their degradation by off-road vehicle use. OPPOSITE TOP: Muddy Creek exits the San Rafael Reef in a dramatic hairpin bend. BOTTOM: Humbug Canyon in the northern San Rafael Swell, with the Book Cliffs rising in the distance.

JEFF GARTON

Utah's West Desert takes in high peaks and broad deserts of the Great Basin Province. Some of these mountain ranges support forests, such as the Granite Peak area shown at right. INSET: Bristlecone pine cling to the steep slopes of the Wah Wah Mountains. In still other ranges, perennial streams harbor rare populations of fishes left over from the last Ice Age.

JEFF GARTON

GREAT BASIN DESERT

Ever since the passage of explorer Jedediah Smith in 1827, Americans have tried to tame, manipulate, and transform the desert into something more to their liking. Failing consistently to civilize it, we call it wasteland.

Mike Medberry
Wilderness at the Edge
(Utah Wilderness Coalition, 1990)

Today, with the pioneers' hardships far behind us, we can begin to appreciate this region's geological and biological marvels. Two dozen mountain ranges rise dramatically out of barren salt flats or vast grasslands, with a vertical relief as great as 7,000 feet. The highest peaks of the Deep Creek Mountains reach over 12,000 feet and support year-round streams and groves of fir and aspen. Several mountain ranges contain ancient bristlecone pine stands. Most of the ranges are not as high, with their upper reaches typically clothed with pinyon pine and juniper.

A less conventional beauty is found in the broad valleys separating the ranges. Here, sagebrush and grasses on the foothills give way to salt-tolerant shrubs, and, lower down, to barren salt flats and seasonal alkali lakes.

Biologists are just beginning to understand the ecological importance of these "island" mountain ranges. Long ago, a cooler and wetter climate allowed plant and animal species to drift between the ranges of the Great Basin. Now, harsh desert separates the mountains, creating ecological islands that still harbor rare species such as the Bonneville cutthroat trout.

SCOTT SMITH

40

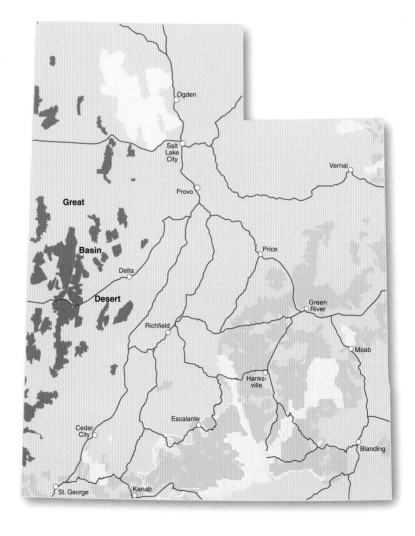

41

OPPOSITE: **The Newfoundland Mountains rise sharply out of the Great Salt Lake Desert. This area was passed over by the BLM and Utah's Congressional Delegation in their wilderness proposals.** ABOVE: **The Barn Hills at the southeastern end of the Confusion Range. Foothills in this and most Great Basin ranges are important year-round habitat for pronghorn antelope (RIGHT).**

42

The key to protecting these species — and perhaps avoiding the need for expensive endangered species recovery efforts — is to protect a full range of remaining habitats. Only the Citizens' Proposal does this, including not only the high peaks of the Deep Creek Mountains and the House Range, but the surrounding benchlands that are important winter range for animals such as pronghorn antelope.

We are also beginning to understand the need for connected wilderness refuges — to allow migration corridors between the desert mountains. Biologists have noticed that in small, isolated refuges, animal species go extinct more easily. The Citizens' Proposal would link up the north-south running mountain ranges by protecting key areas such as King Top Mountain, which is left out of other wilderness proposals.

OPPOSITE: The San Francisco Mountains northwest of Milford. Mine workings dot the southern end of these mountains but a roadless tract remains in its northern portion. TOP: The Pilot Range straddles the Utah-Nevada border north of Wendover. LEFT: Evening shadows in the Thomas Range, part of a chain of mountains straddling the Pony Express route.

43

44

The wild Dome Plateau country
northeast of Moab looks
across the canyon of the
Colorado River to Castleton
Tower and the La Sal
Mountains. With human
visitation exploding in the
Moab area, it becomes
essential to protect areas still
remote from highways, roads
and visitor centers. INSET:
Pictograph in a tributary to
Labyrinth Canyon. A visitor
who has floated fifty miles down
this gentle wilderness river is
not likely to vandalize such a
priceless rock art panel. If a
road were built to the site, it
would not be as safe.

TOM TILL

TOM TILL

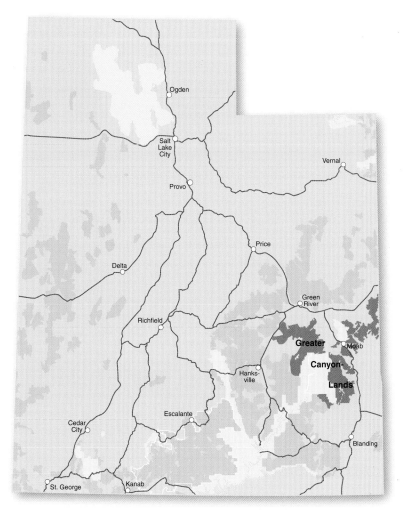

GREATER CANYONLANDS

In 1964, Congress established Canyonlands National Park, securing protection for 258,000 acres of spectacular redrock country centering on the confluence of the Green and Colorado rivers. But that action was a compromise with user groups of the day. Original proposals for the park were much larger, taking in the Orange Cliffs to the west, the Dark Canyon Plateau to the south, and the rugged mesas to the east. Expansion of the park to 338,000 acres in 1971 still left much of this country unprotected.

Publicly owned wild lands that were left out of the park have not fared well under BLM management. In the last three decades, energy companies have built roads and cleared drillpads throughout the area. The clamor for tourist highways has led to the paving of roads to scenic overlooks. Off-road vehicles have scarred hillsides, and protection for archeological resources has been lacking.

Within the greater Canyonlands region are found roadless wild land complexes in Labyrinth Canyon, Dark Canyon, Canyonlands Basin, and Behind the Rocks. North and east of Moab lie additional wild lands surrounding the La Sal Mountains and along the Colorado River's Westwater Canyon.

The Citizens' Proposal for America's Redrock Wilderness seeks to establish a balance between consumptive uses and preservation on the public lands surrounding Canyonlands. By keeping all of the remaining roadless BLM lands intact, we would protect the remainder of this once seamless wild region.

OPPOSITE: **Tower at Hatch Point on BLM lands at the edge of Canyonlands National Park.** TOP: **Anasazi ruin on BLM public lands.** BOTTOM: **Dragonfly in Negro Bill Canyon.**

47

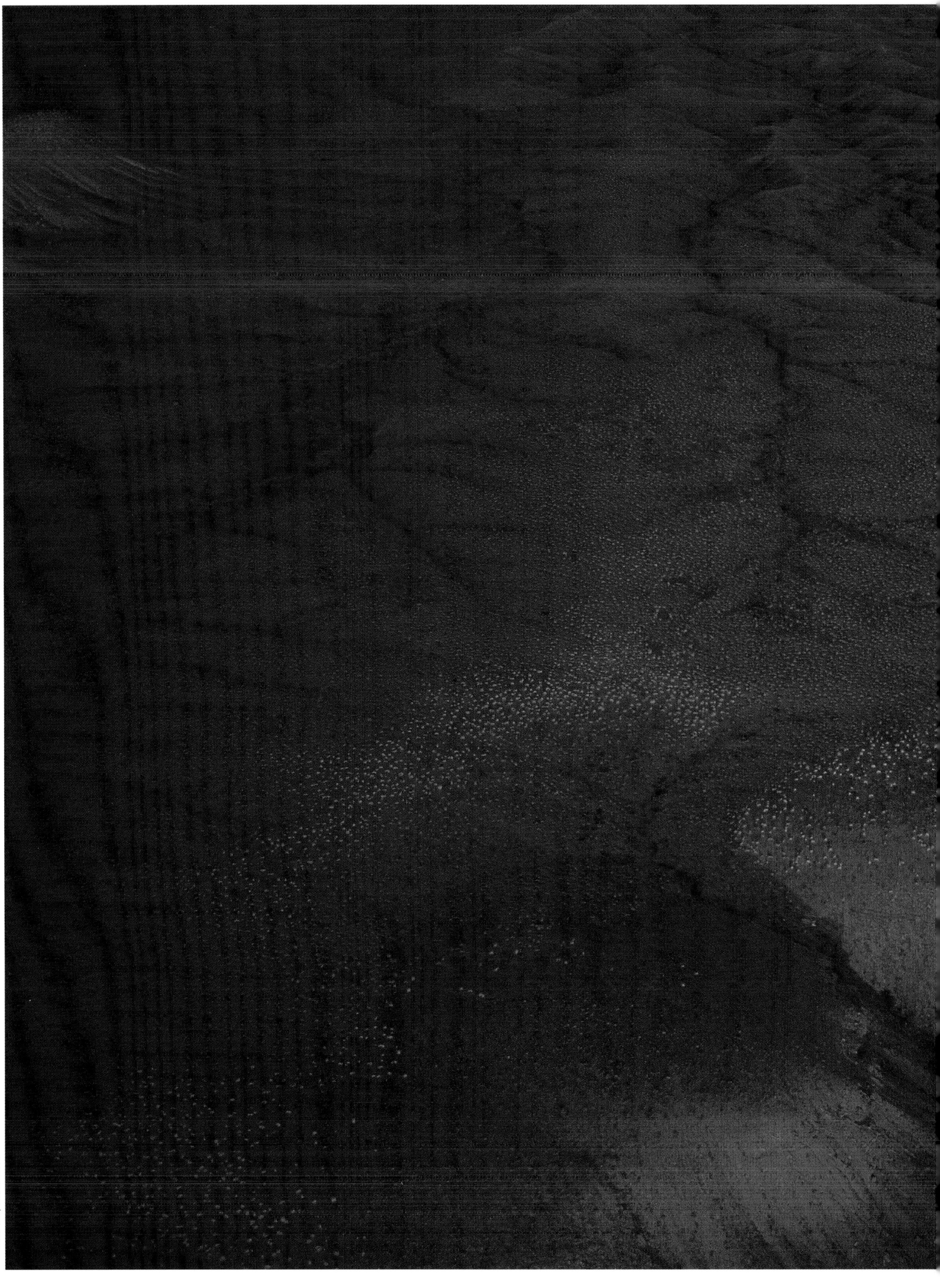

TOM TILL/LIGHTHAWK

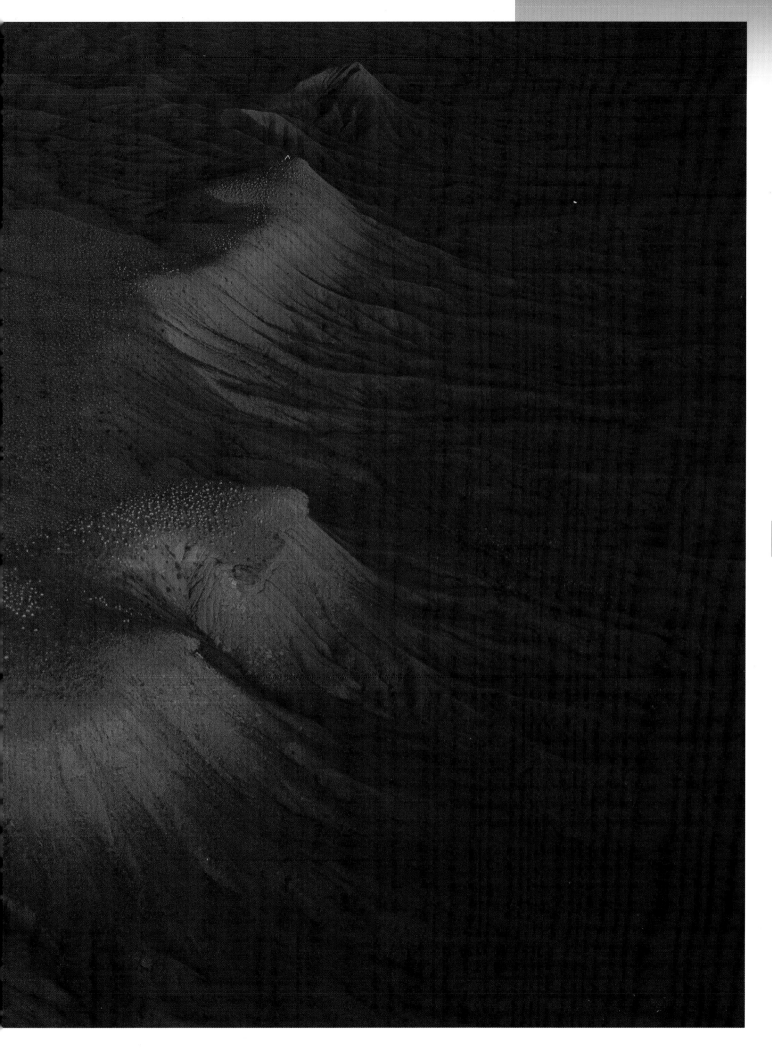

JIM CATLIN

JOHN P. GEORGE

Book Cliffs - Uinta Basin

BOOK CLIFFS AND UINTA BASIN

In the fractious debate over Utah's public lands, the Book Cliffs enjoys a remarkable consensus: nearly everyone agrees that this region's remarkable big game herds must be protected.

Containing half of the vertebrate species found in Utah, the Book Cliffs and the million acres of mostly undeveloped land to the north represent a rare opportunity. Worldwide biological research has shown the importance of large, unfragmented areas of wildlife habitat. The larger the undisturbed area, the greater the number of species it can support — and the less likely they are to be threatened by human and environmental changes.

The Bureau of Land Management lands in the Book Cliffs and Uinta Basin are the keystone to the whole region. The BLM manages the least-developed lands, having some of the highest wildlife values. Roadless area protection for these lands is crucial to the success of region-wide conservation efforts.

To date, the BLM has allowed hydrocarbon exploration and development in many parts of this roadless region. The Citizens' Proposal excludes these developed areas, but carefully draws the line at further encroachments into Utah's greatest single wild region.

51

PREVIOUS: **Sunset illuminates badland hills at the base of the Book Cliffs east of Crescent Junction.** OPPOSITE: **Nearby impenetrable ridges and valleys define much of the Book Cliffs wilderness.** TOP: **The White River south of Vernal offers an easy canoe trip through wild country often visited by migrating waterfowl.** LEFT: **The high forested plateaus of the Book Cliffs region are home to large elk herds.**

Wild Mercy

We are at a crease in history where we must decide as human beings if we want to sustain our relationship to wild places. In the American West, we want to possess, to control, to remain sovereigns against the political pull of the East. We raise clenched fists to the wind. We are still afraid of wildness: wild places, wild acts, wild thoughts. But if we were to bring our hands down in the gesture of a prayer, perhaps we would find that the source of our humanity lies in our restraint, our compassion, our ability to imagine living in accordance with nature.

"We are not debating 'wilderness' here in trying to decide the fate of Utah's undeveloped public lands," writes Barry Lopez. "The term is too restrictive. We're debating the future direction of Western civilization . . . . A brutal, pointed lesson of human history is that unhealthy civilizations die. Civilizations that are physically, spiritually or economically corrosive fall apart. Their people wither. If we do not want to pass away as a civilization, let alone as a Western nation . . . . We need to see what a grave decision the release of public land for development is."

We have a chance to do something fine and brave and visionary. There are still vast expanses of wild country in Utah, country that supports mountain lions, black bears, elk, deer and bobcats. It is a tapestry of plant life that has much to teach us about adaptation. It is a desert draped by beautiful rivers where a thirst for water is matched by a thirst for beauty and solitude. It is rugged terrain the color of blood where turkey vultures waver on heat waves that blister our skin. The Colorado Plateau is an acquired taste.

We can protect these lands, secure them for the future, keep them whole as they keep us sane. This is not about economics. This is not a rift between environmentalists and the preservation of ranching culture in the American West. And it is especially not about settling a political feud once and for all. This is a call for redrock democracy.

As Americans, we must ask ourselves, "Can we really survive the worship of our own destructiveness?" Who can say how much land can be used for extractive purposes until it is rendered barren forever? And who can say what the human spirit will be crying out for one hundred years from now?

The eyes of the future are looking back at us and they are praying for us to see beyond our own time. Our descendants are kneeling with clasped hands hoping we might act with restraint, that we might leave room for the life that is destined to come. To protect what is wild is to protect what is gentle. Perhaps the wilderness we fear is the pause between our own heartbeats, the silence that reminds us we live only by grace. Wilderness lives by this same grace. It is within our legislative power to create merciful laws. Can we say the word "mercy" when speaking about the land? Can we minimize harm to others, our own species and beyond?

I am a fifth generation Utahn. When Brigham Young looked across the Great Salt Lake Valley in 1847 and declared, "This is the place," there are those of us who still believe him. Our family has made its living for four generations by laying pipe in the substrate of Utah. We have benefitted financially by the state's capacity to grow and we have contributed to that growth by our own numbers. But there comes a time when we must ask ourselves, "What sustains a quality of life?" For our family, the quality of our lives is in direct proportion to time spent in the natural world. This is what sustains us physically, emotionally, and spiritually.

Wilderness is not an extravagance or a luxury, it is a place of original memory where we can witness and reflect on how the world is held together by natural laws. It is a landscape of humility. Our shared love for the land brings us home, again and again. It seems simplistic to say we cannot bear to see this unusual country ruthlessly maimed, dammed, drilled or developed. But we can't. And it is. We stand before these remaining acres in a compromised state. We ask for the remote canyons, buttes and mesas of southern Utah to be protected. They hold our stories, our dreams, our deepest secrets. Utah's wilderness is one of the last strongholds of peace. It is a large part of why we choose to live here and it is certainly why we stay. These lands are public. They will disarm you. They swing the doors of our imagination wide open.

— Terry Tempest Williams

The Southern Utah Wilderness Alliance (SUWA), with 20,000 members nationwide, is working to protect the incomparable redrock canyons and deserts of southern Utah. As a charter member of the Utah Wilderness Coalition, we work with 155 other local, regional and national organizations to secure wilderness designation for qualifying Bureau of Land Management public lands in Utah.

We invite your support. Membership dues are $30.

Contact us at:
SUWA
1471 South 1100 East
Salt Lake City, Utah 84105
(801) 486-3161

215 Pennsylvania Ave. S.E.
3rd Floor
Washington, D.C. 20003
(202) 546-2215

Email: suwa@suwa.org

Webpage: http://www.suwa.org/

We wish to thank the Mennen Environmental Foundation and our members for supporting the publication of this brochure. Thanks also to the photographers who kindly donated their work.

Quotations on page 6 by Donald Snow and on page 52 by Barry Lopez are from *Testimony: Writers of the West Speak Out on Behalf of Utah Wilderness*, complied by Stephen Trimble and Terry Tempest Williams (Milkweed Editions, 1996). Robert Marshall quotation on page 7 is cited in *The Big Outside*, by Dave Foreman and Howie Wolke. (Ned Ludd Books, 1989). Quotations on page 11 by Ward Roylance are from *The Enchanted Wilderness, A Red Rock Odyssey* by Ward J. Roylance (Four Corners West, 1986).

DESIGN BY EASTON DESIGN GROUP

PRINTED IN HONG KONG

STEPHEN TRIMBLE